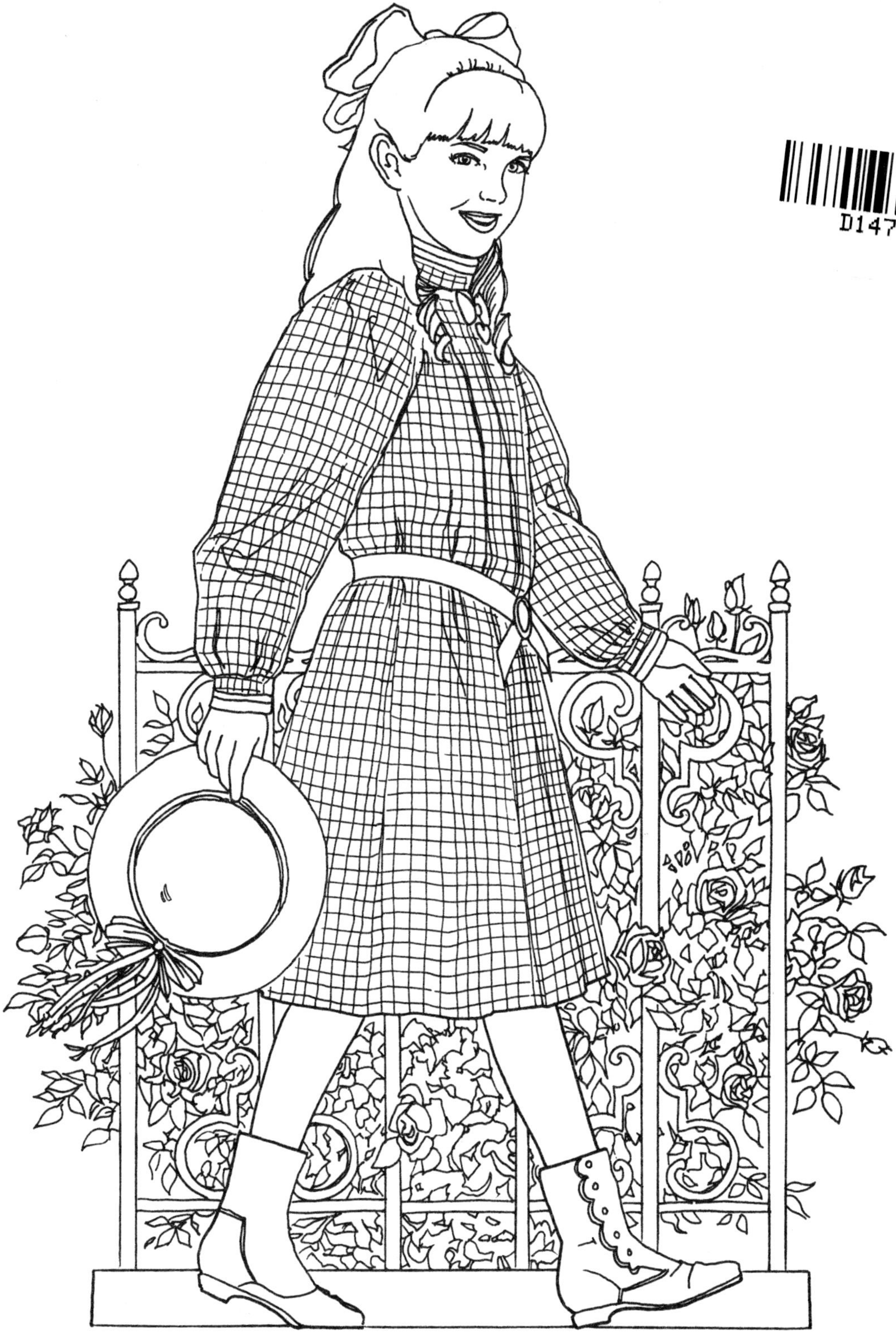

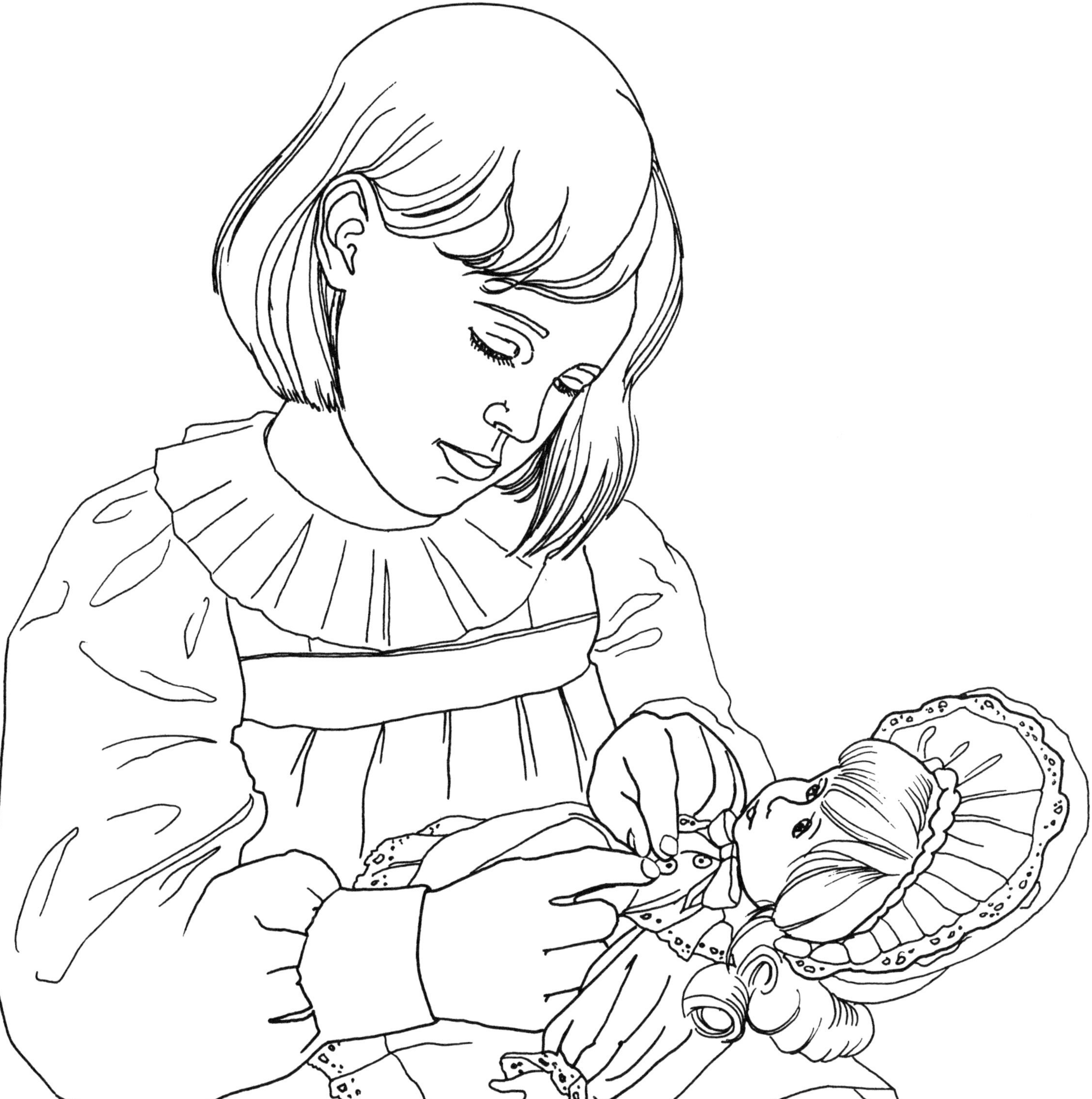

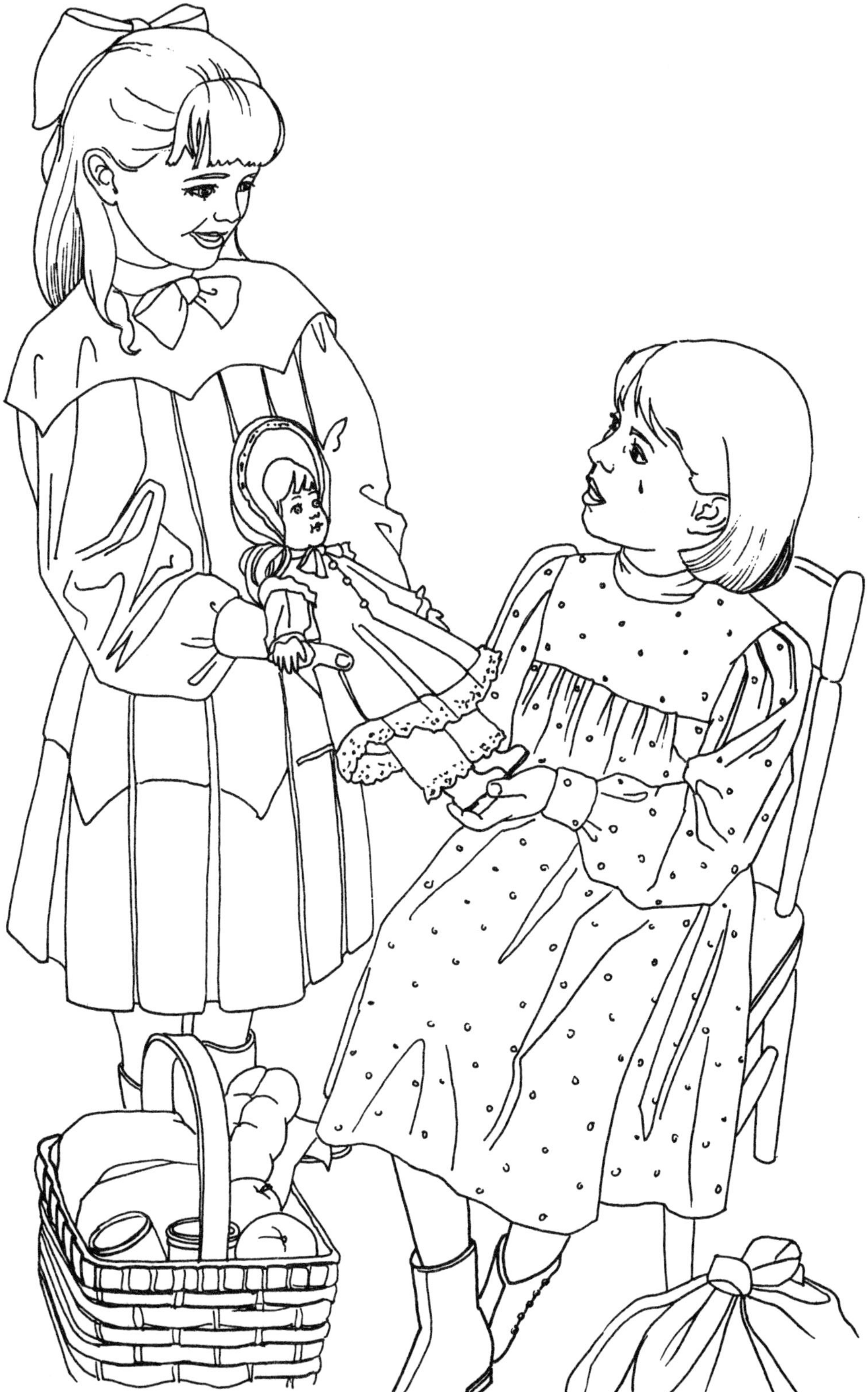

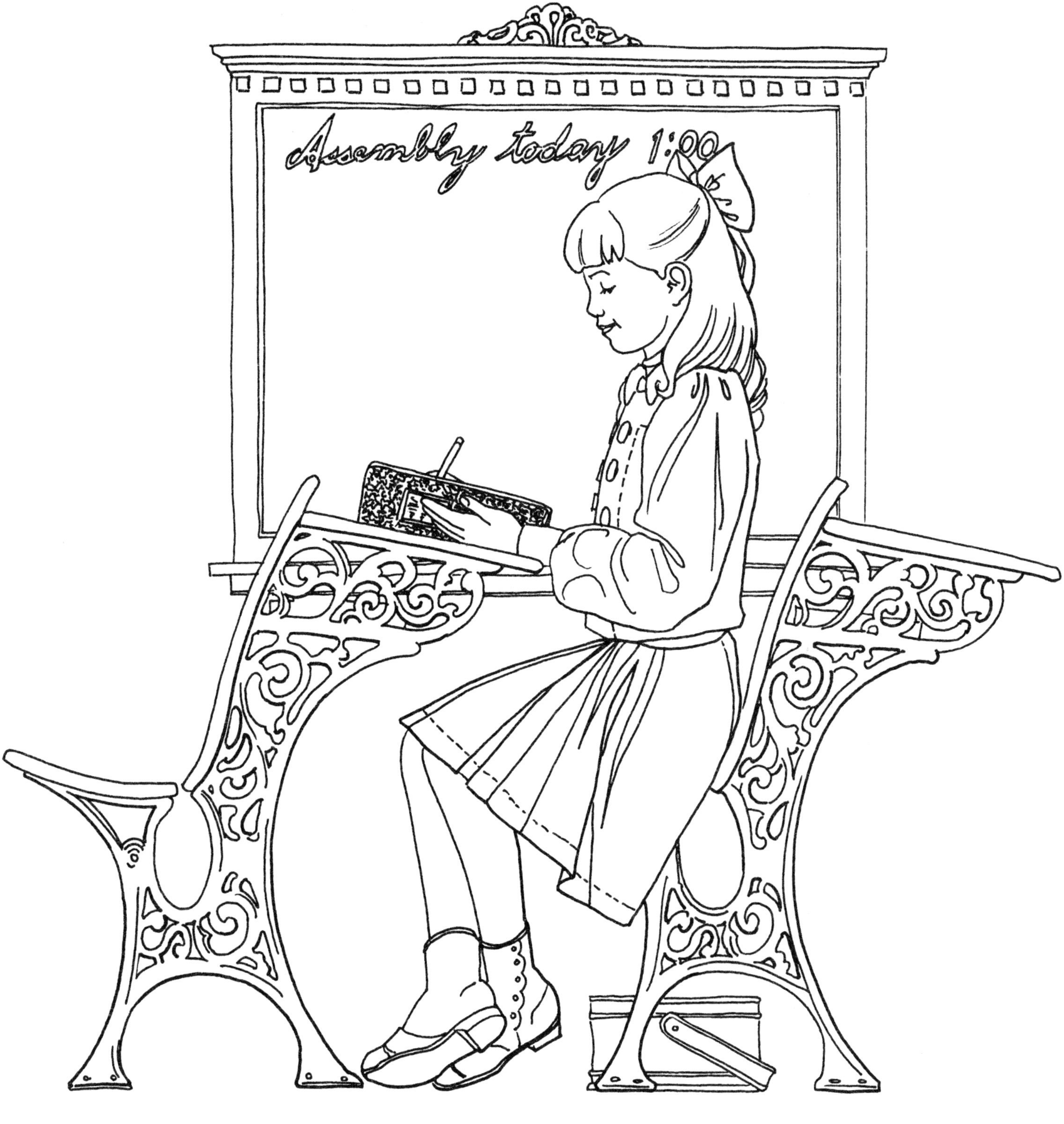
Assembly today 1:00

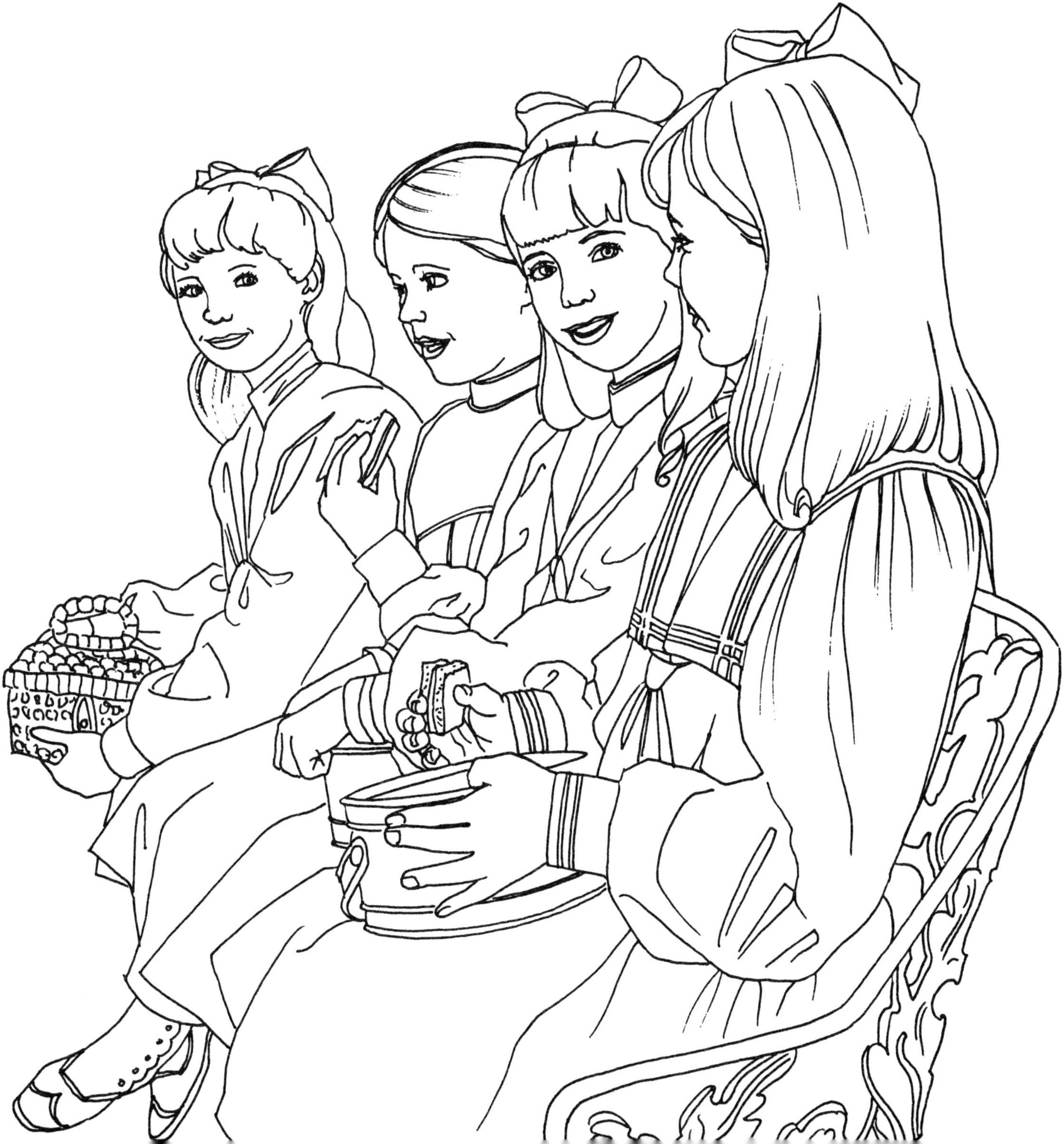

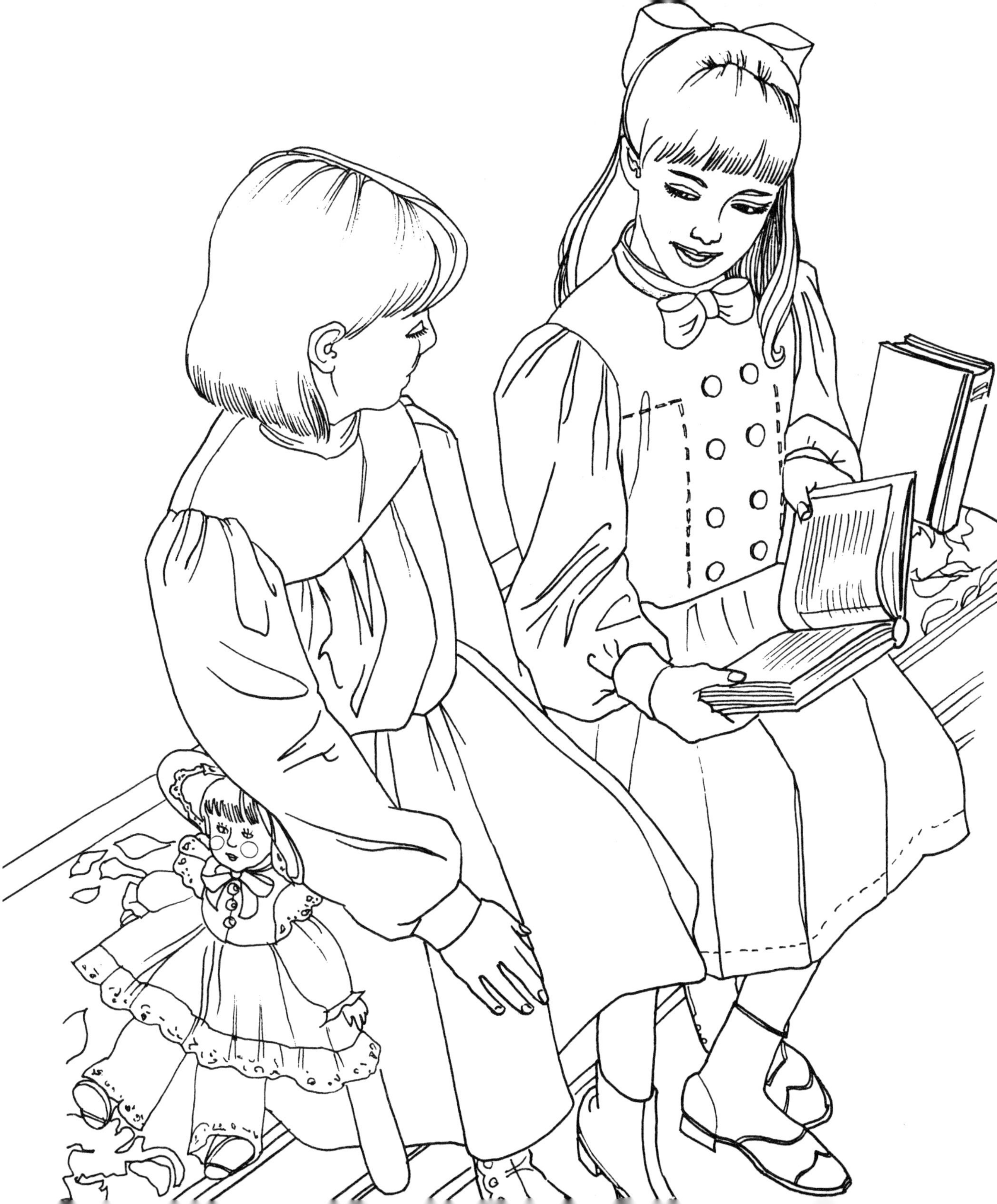

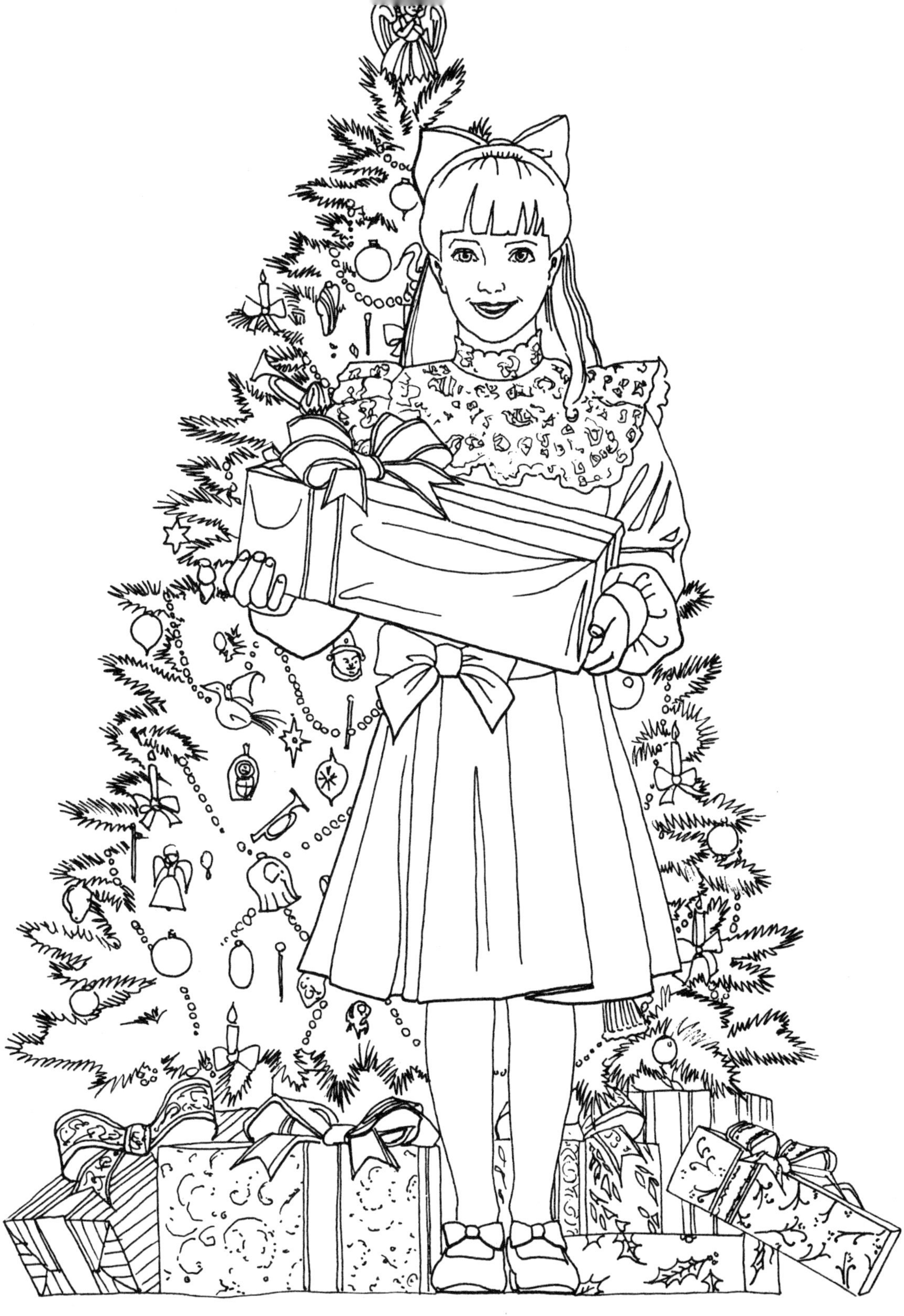

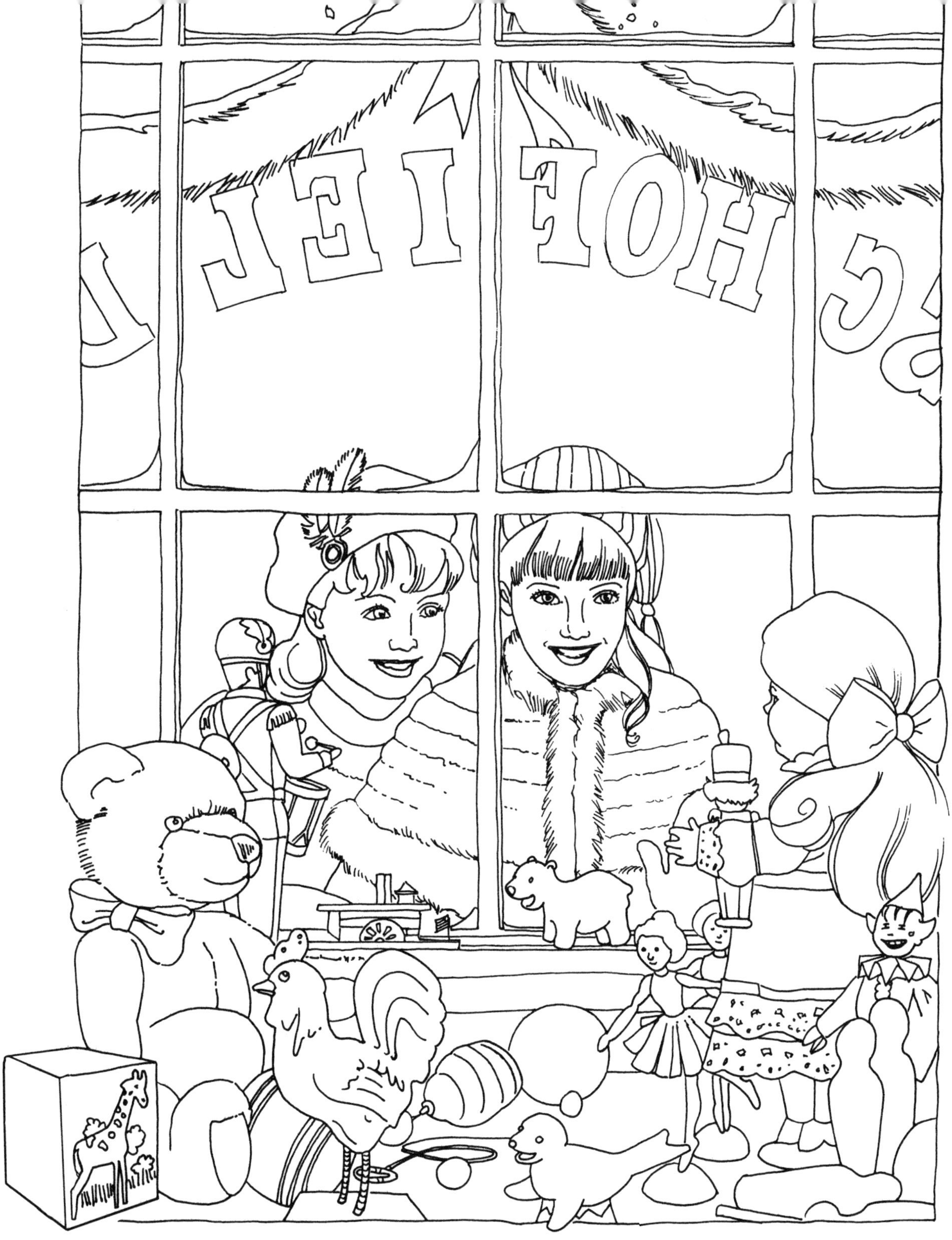

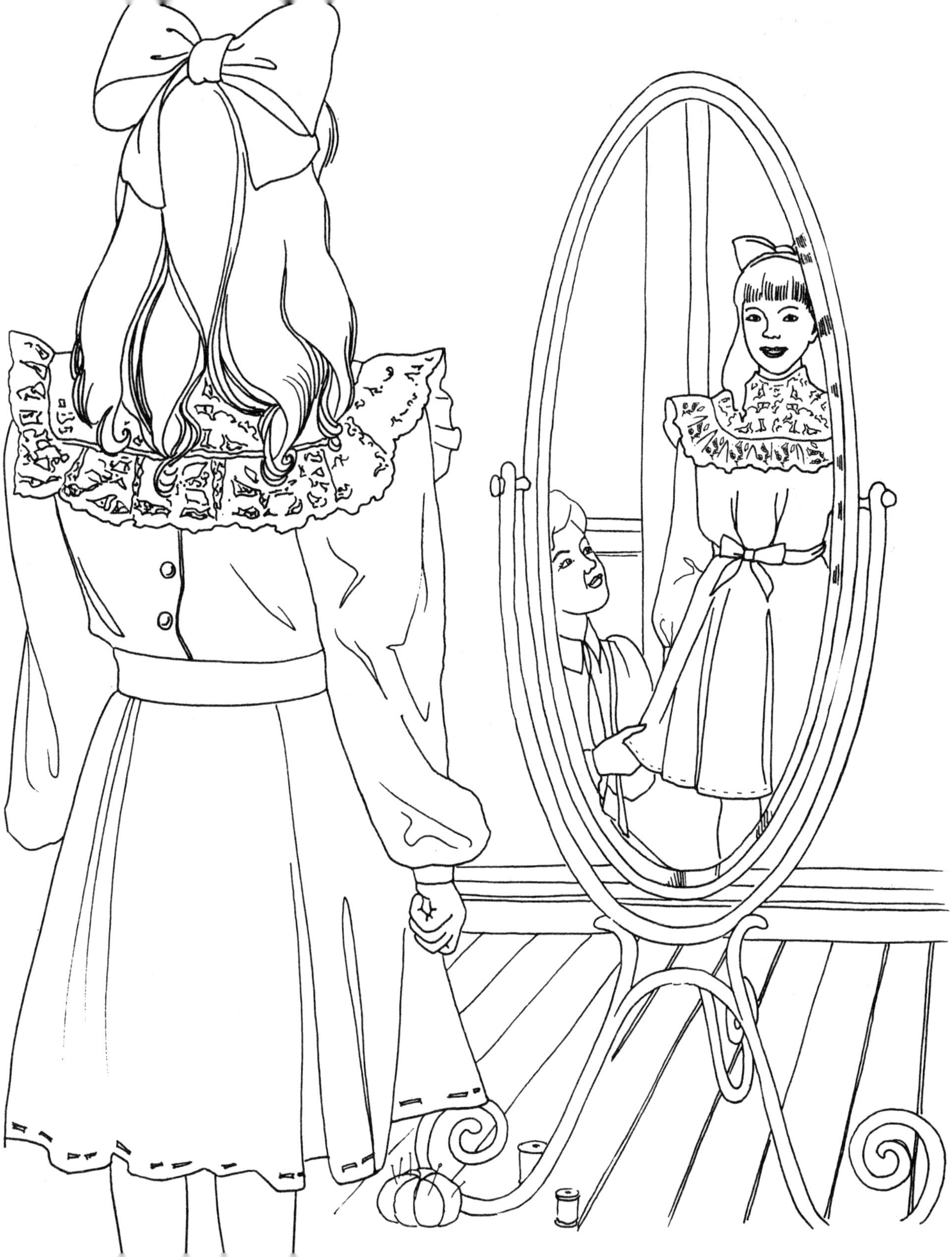

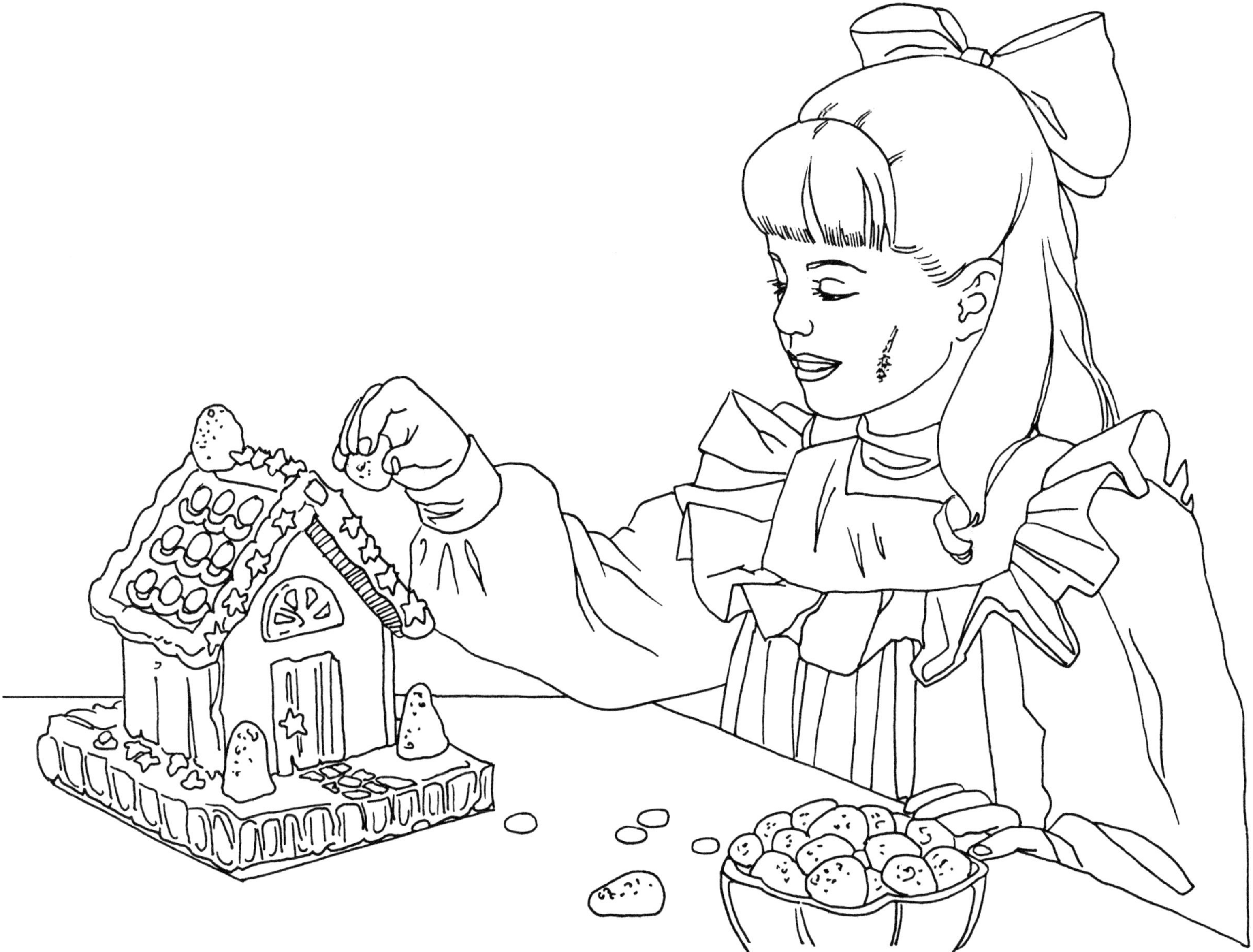

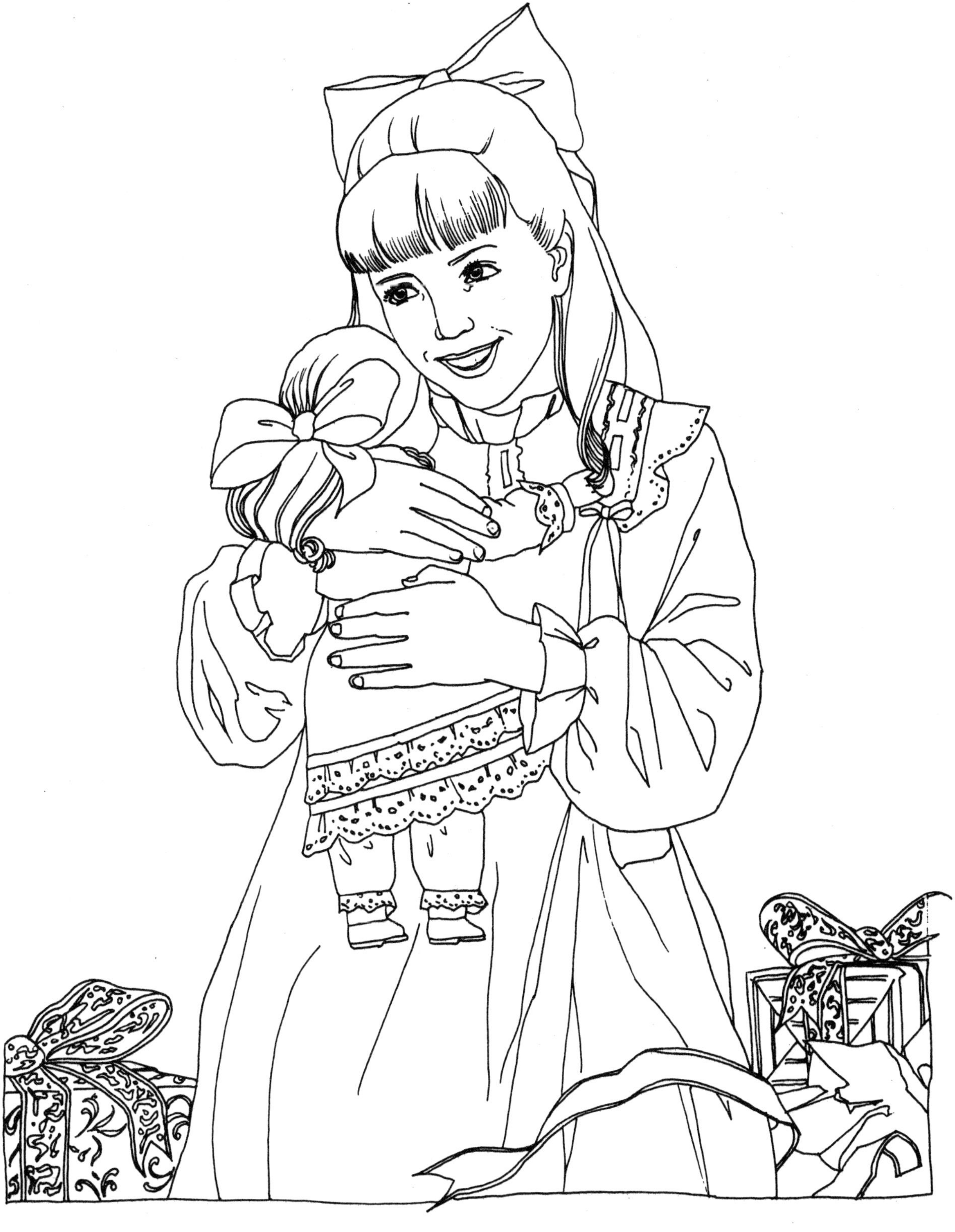

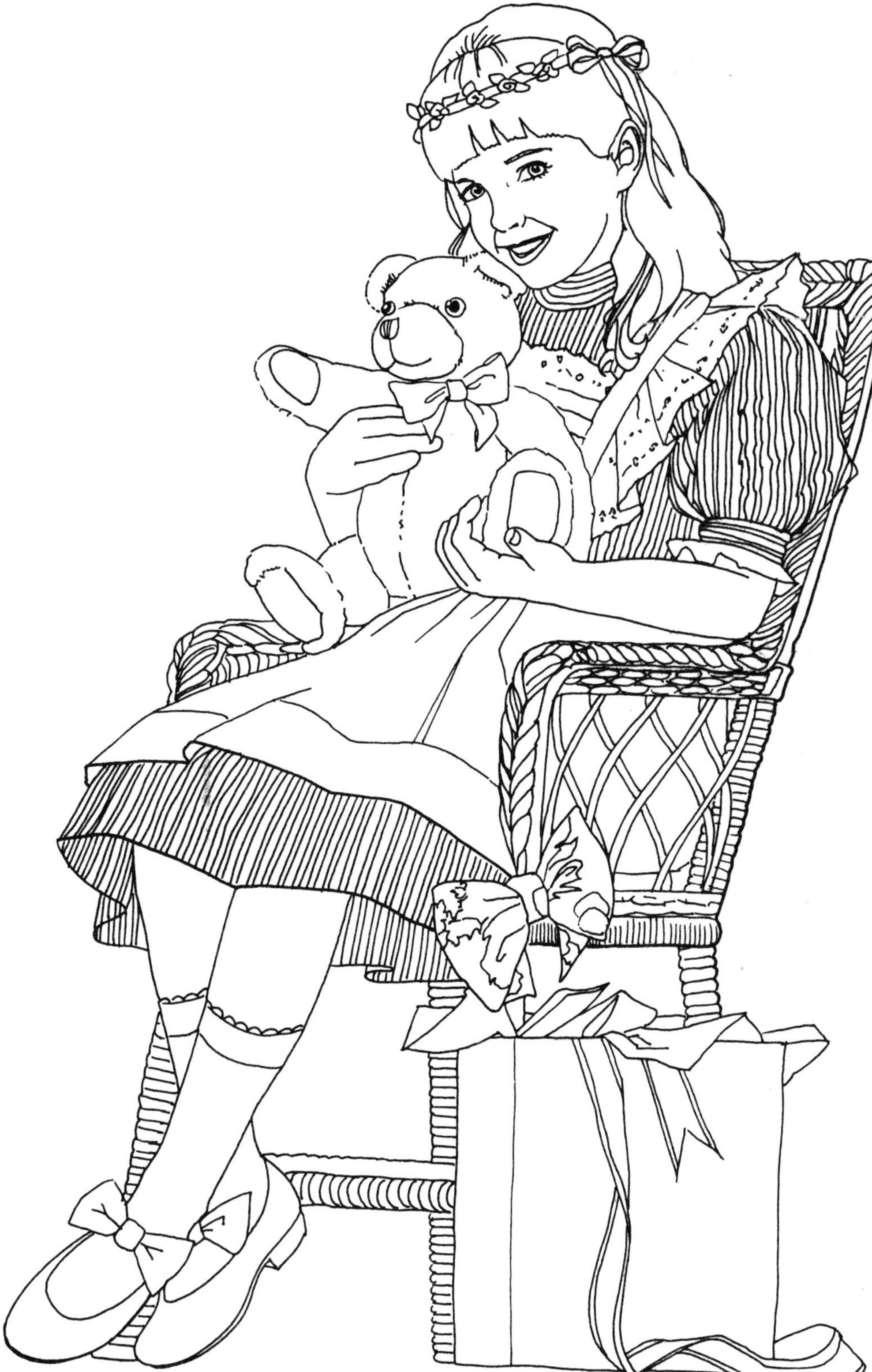

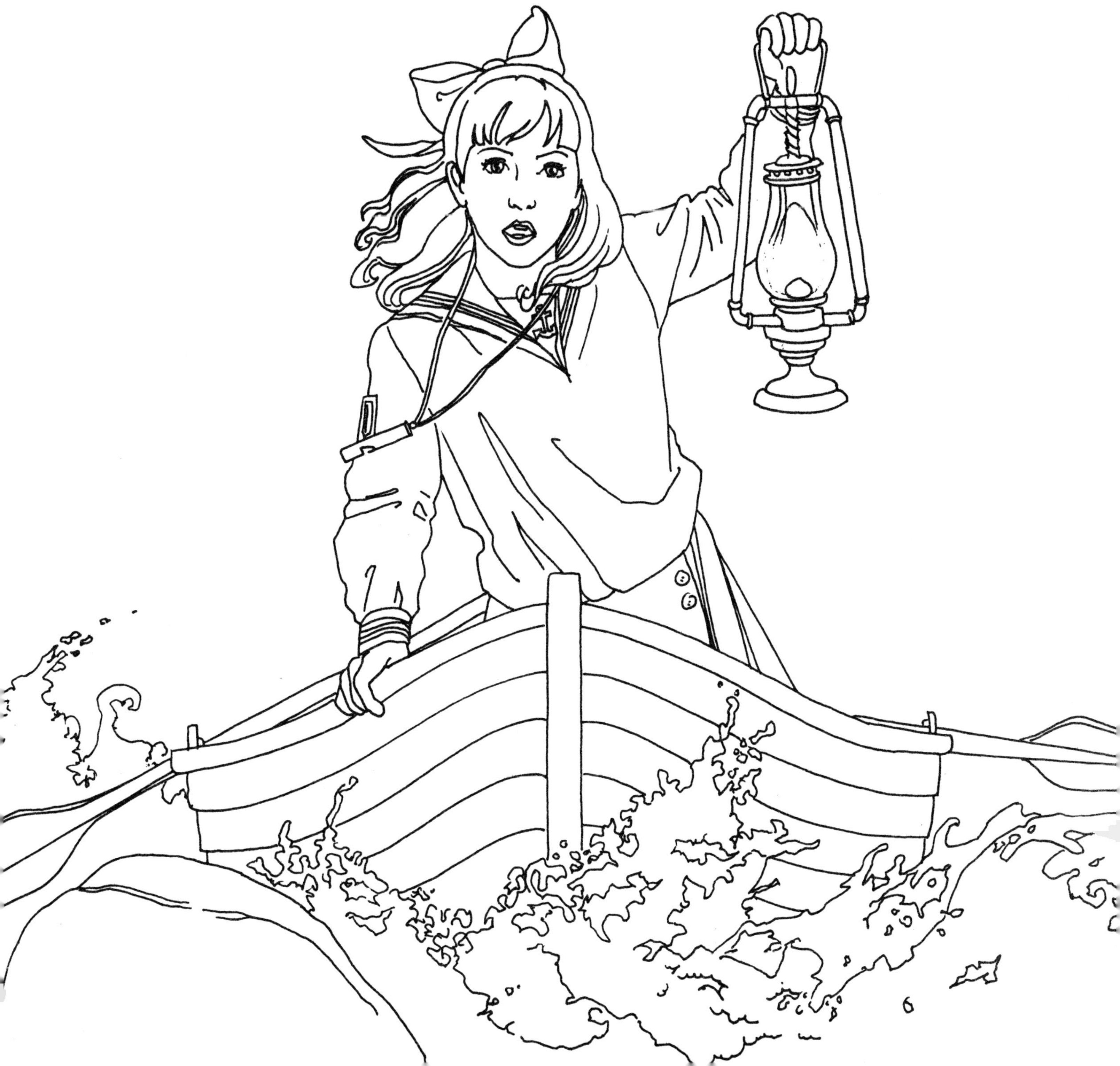

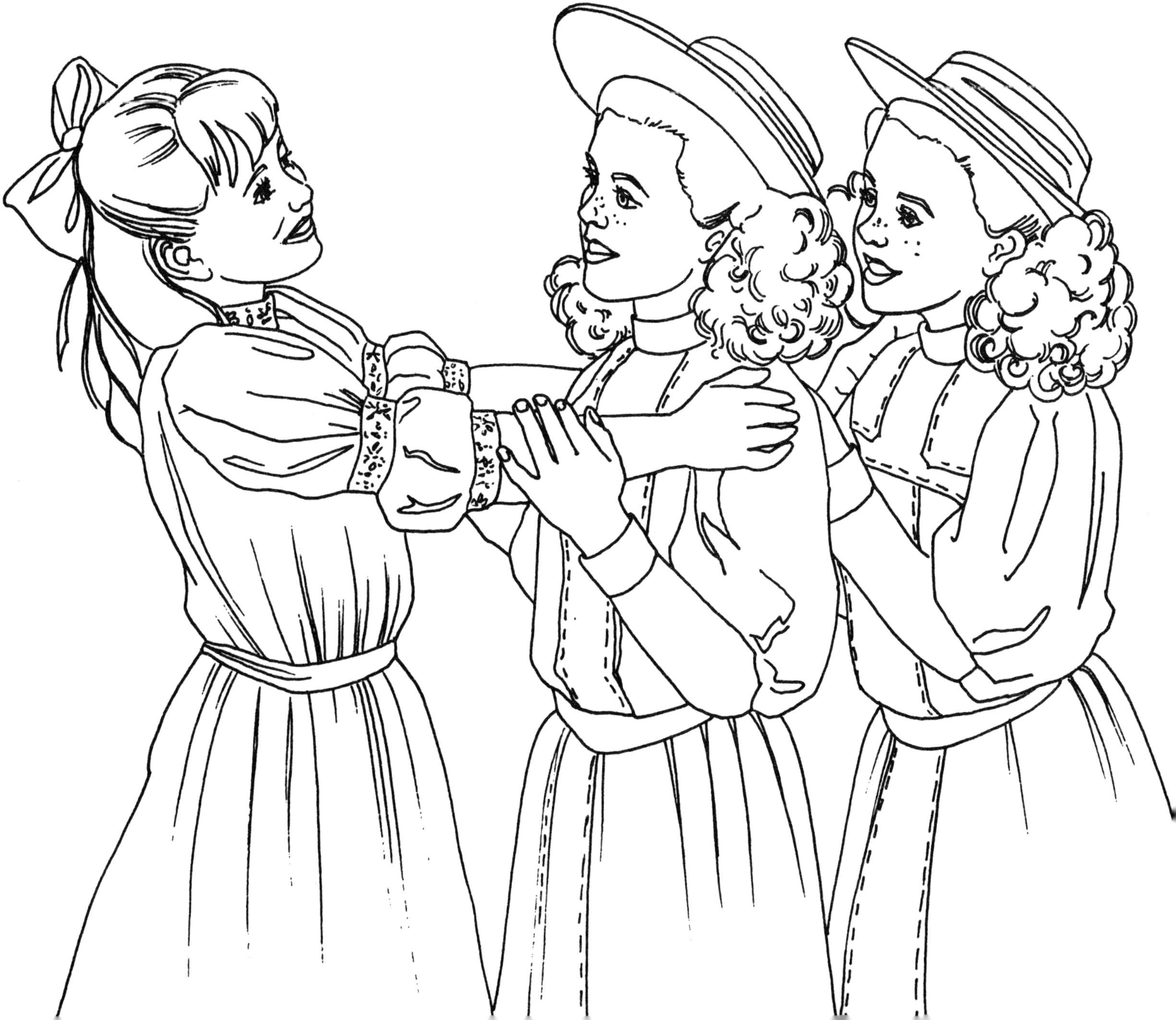

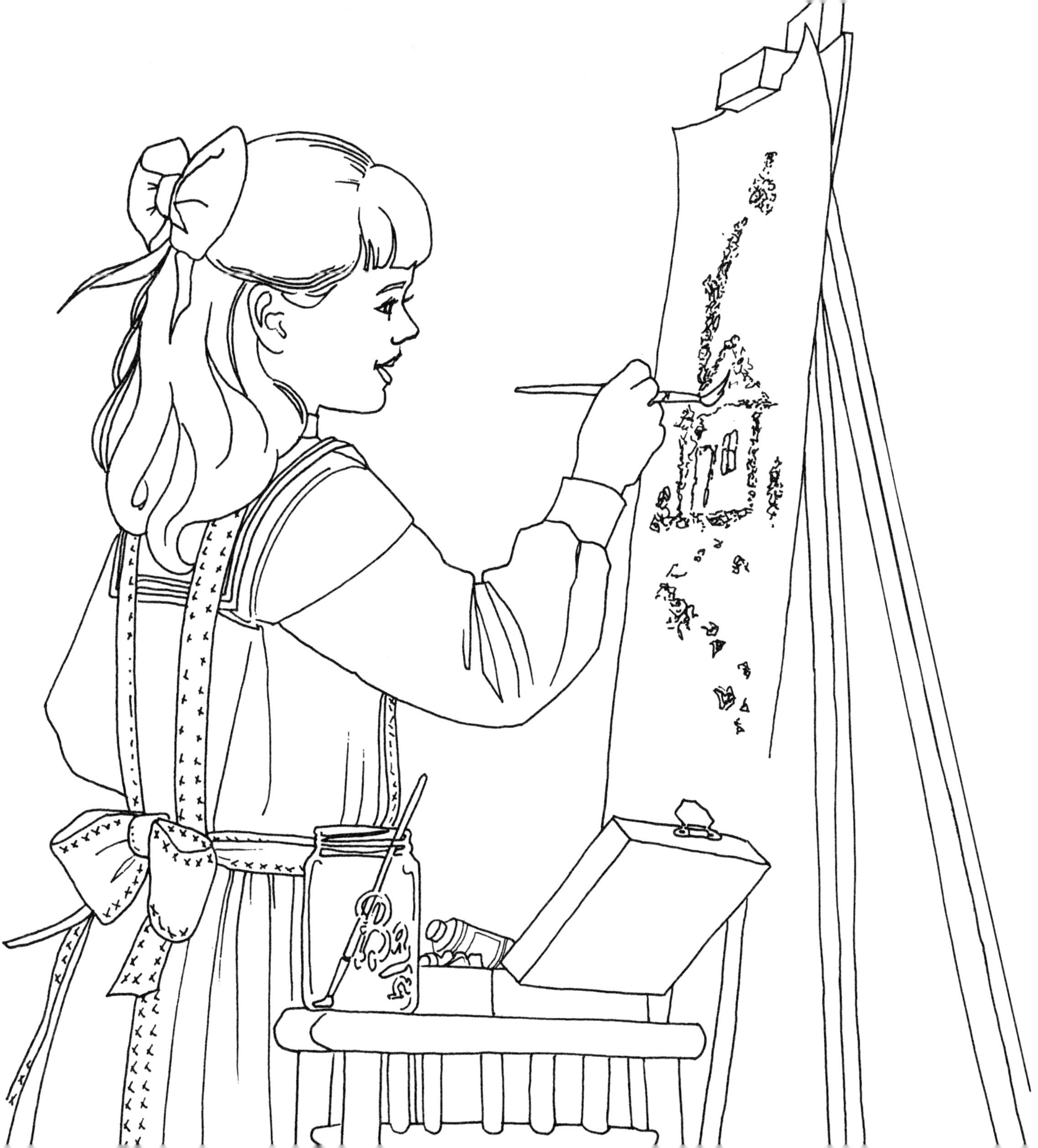

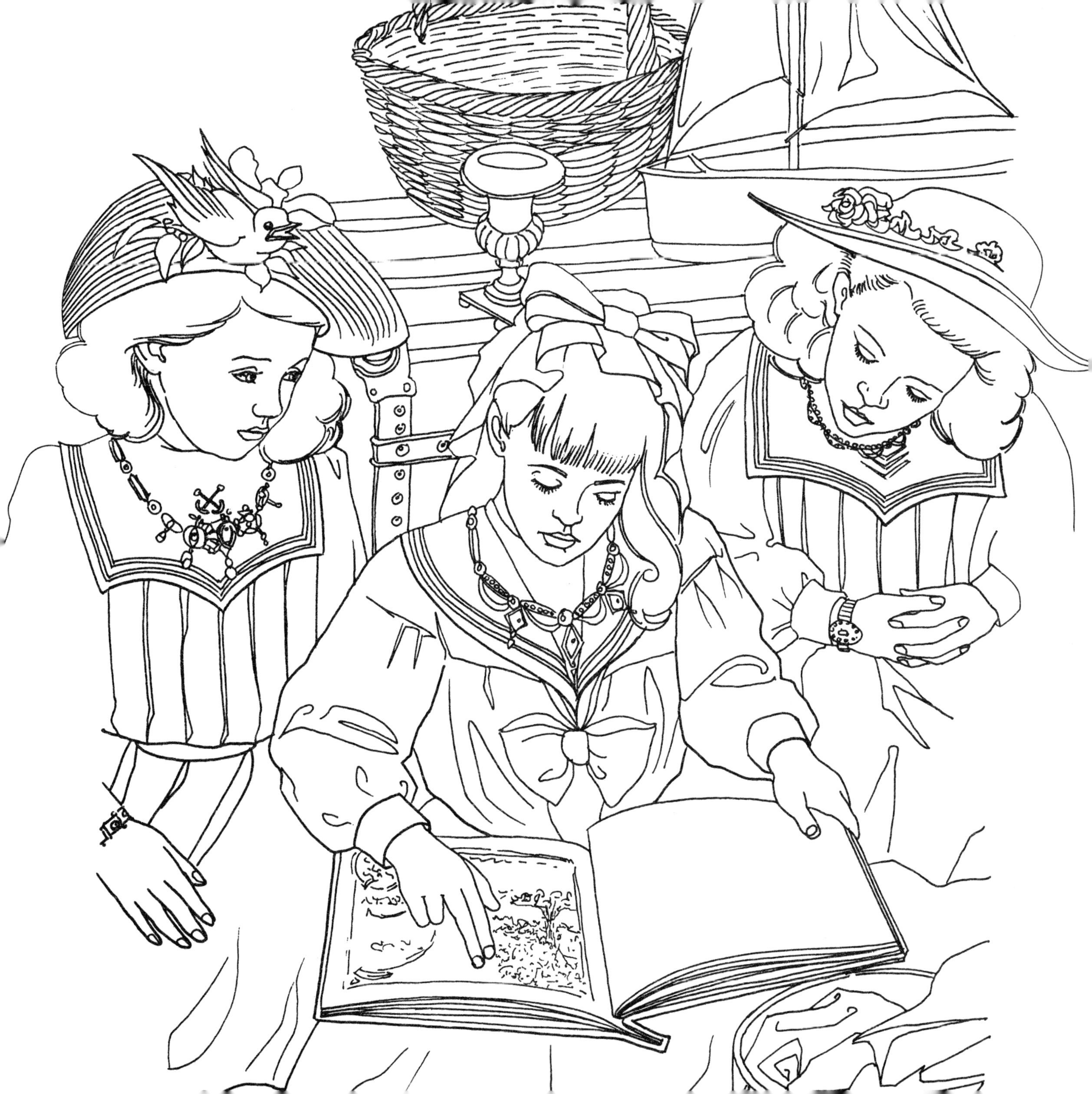

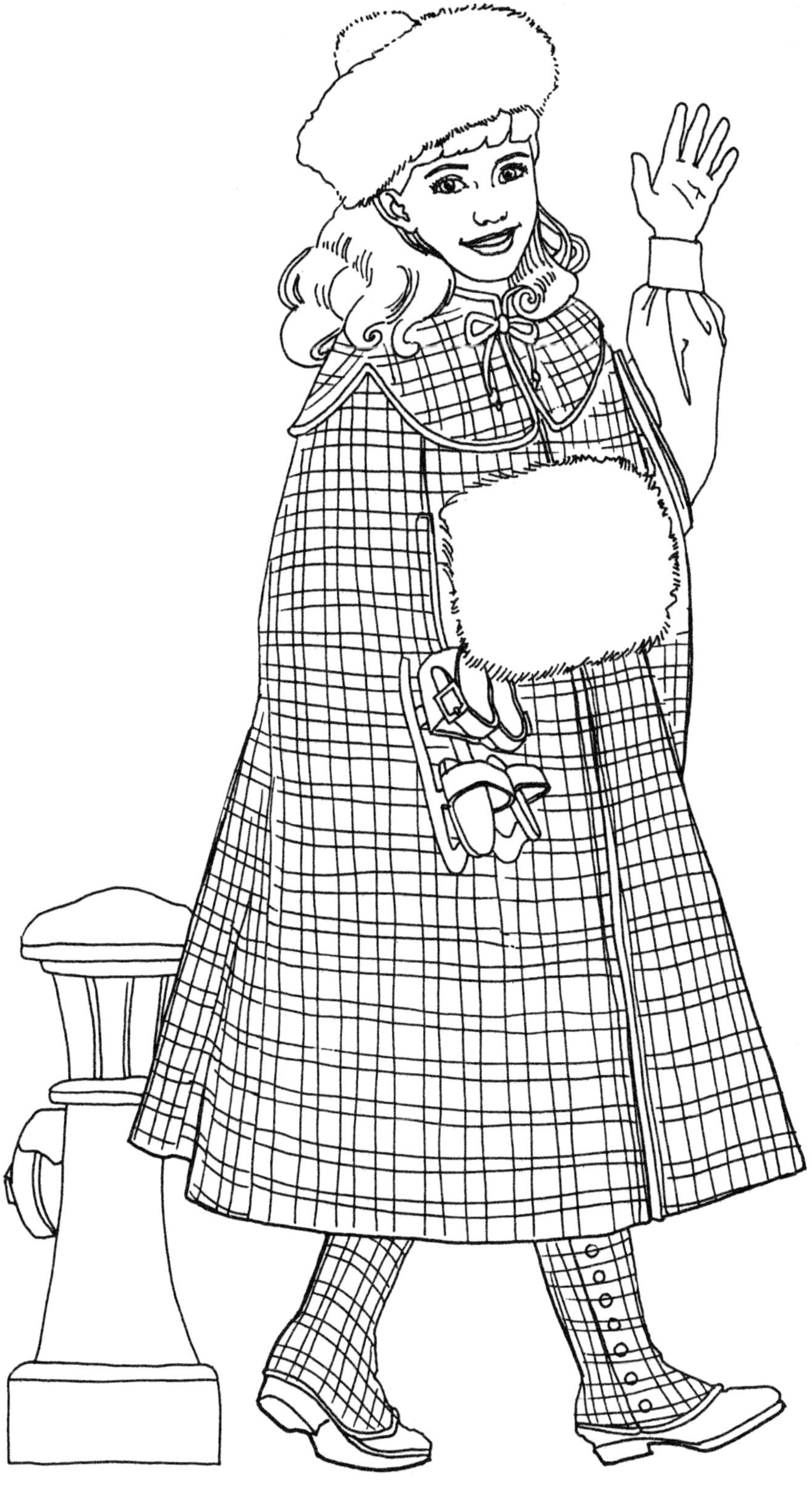

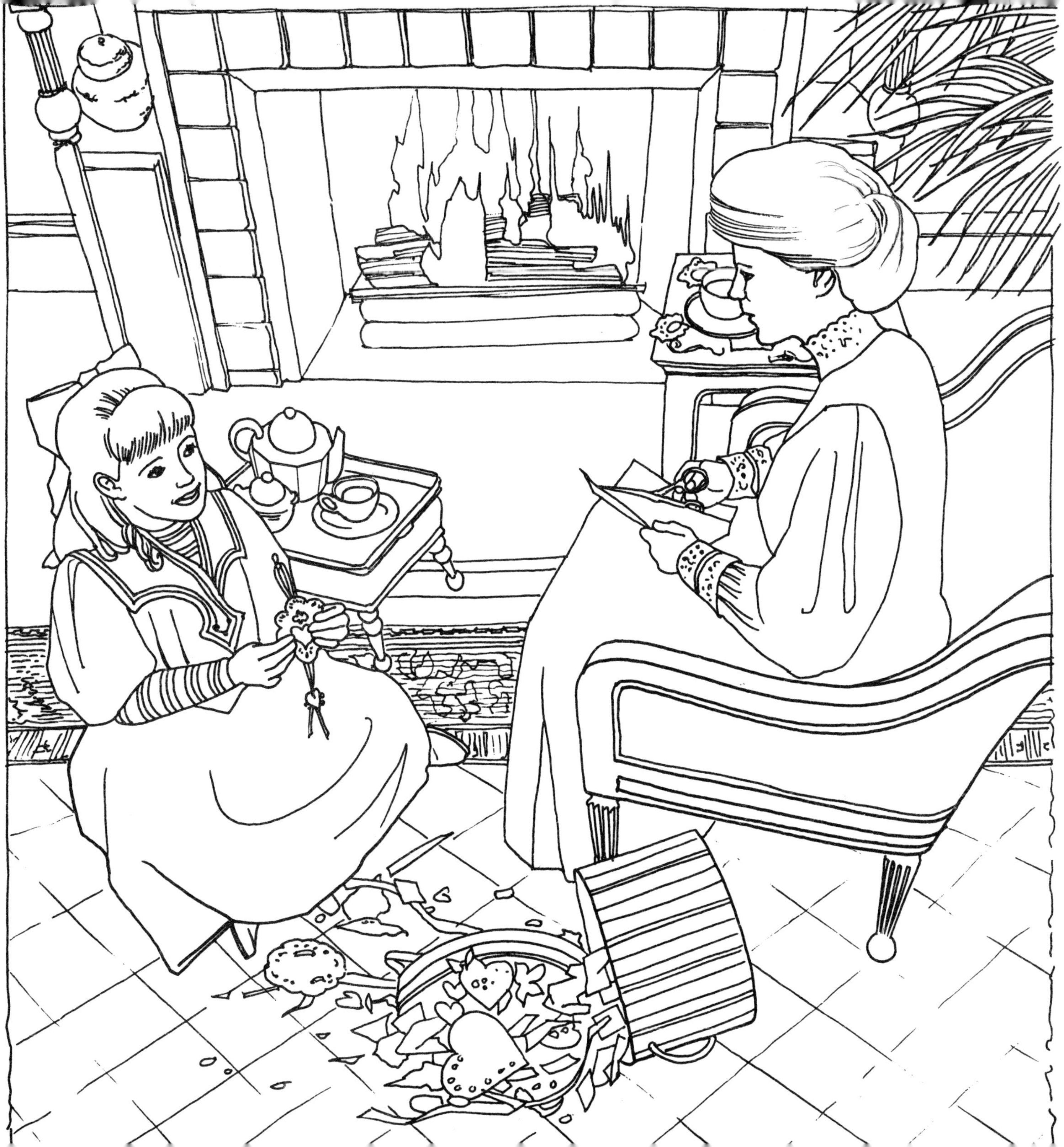

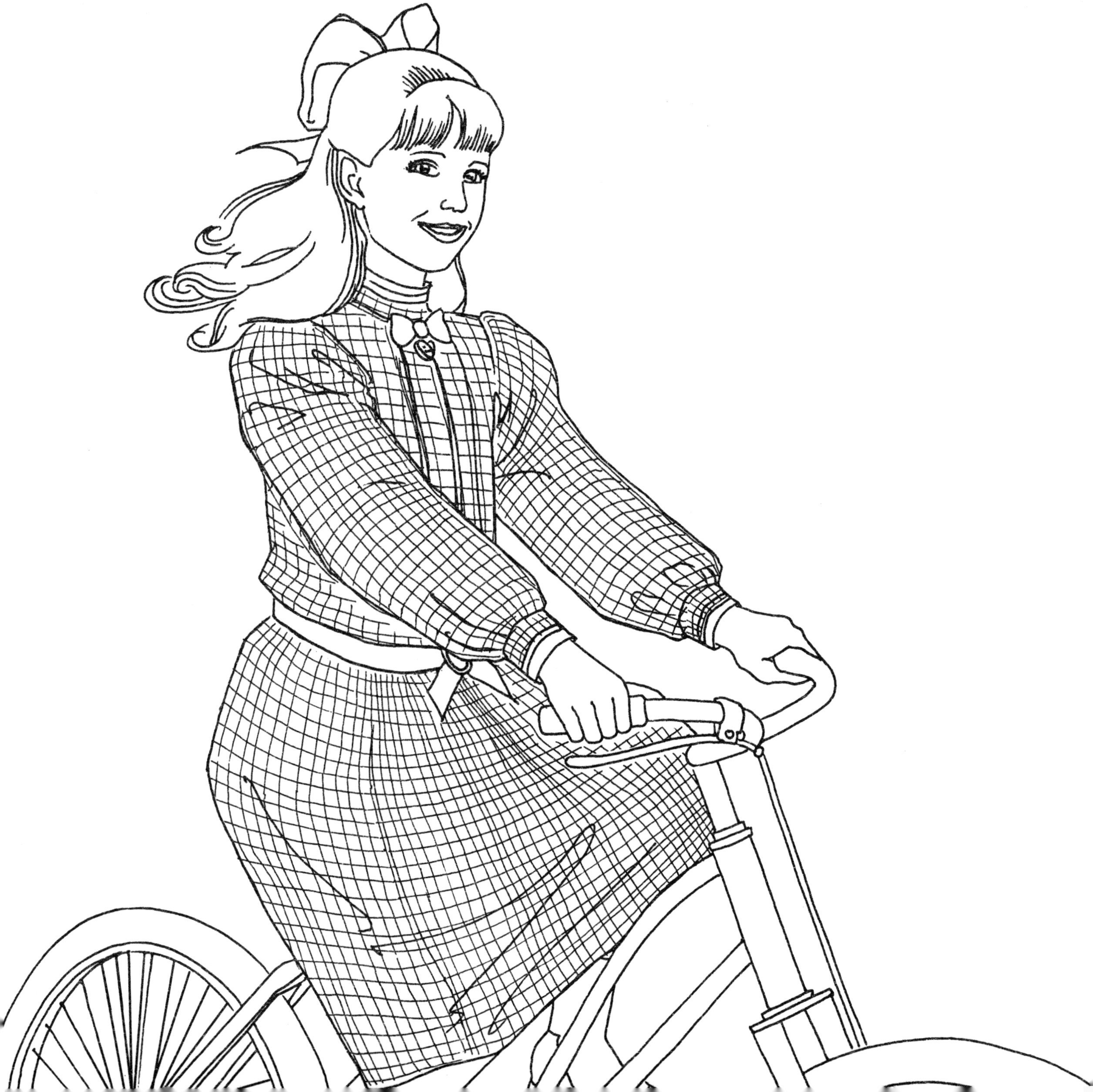

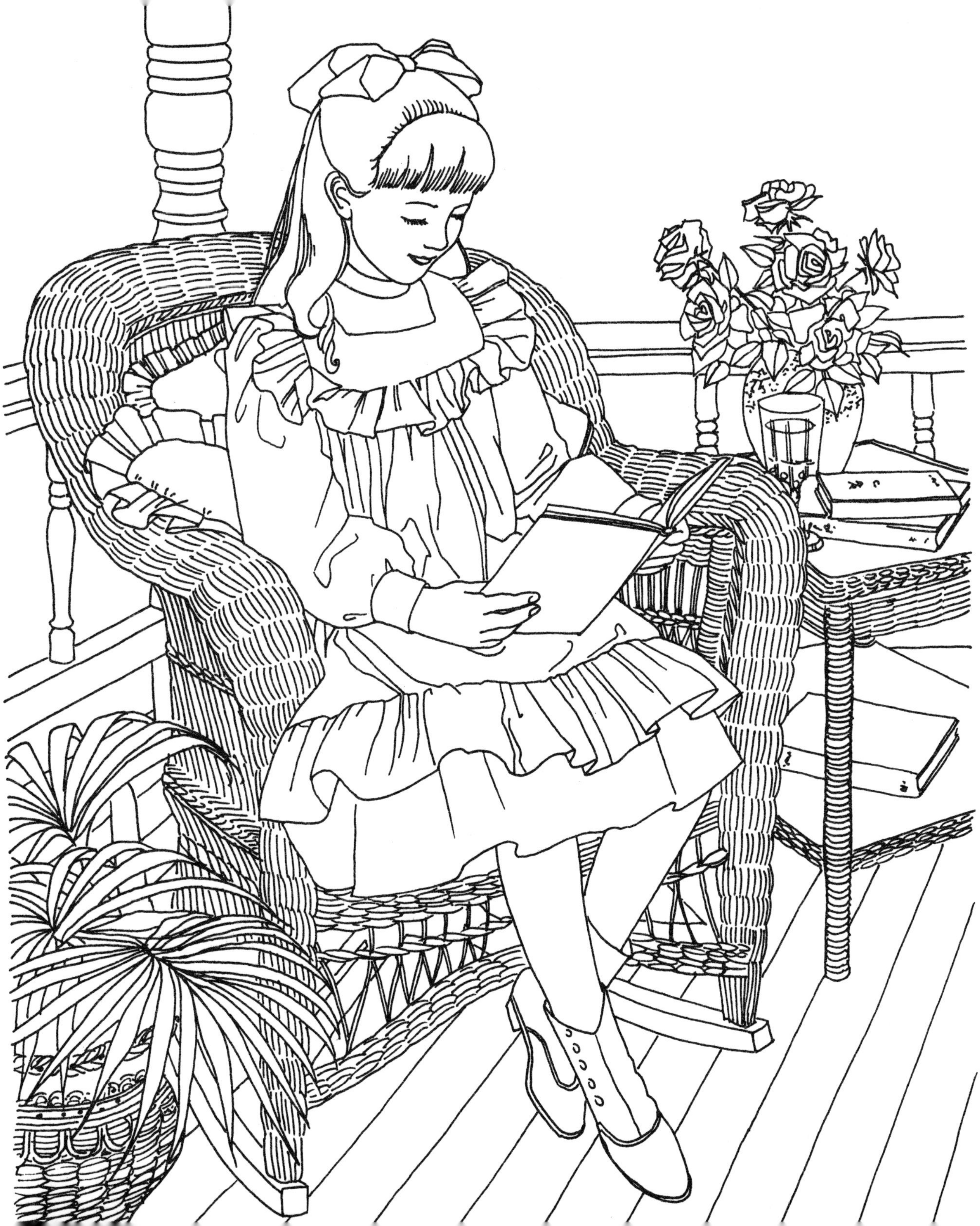

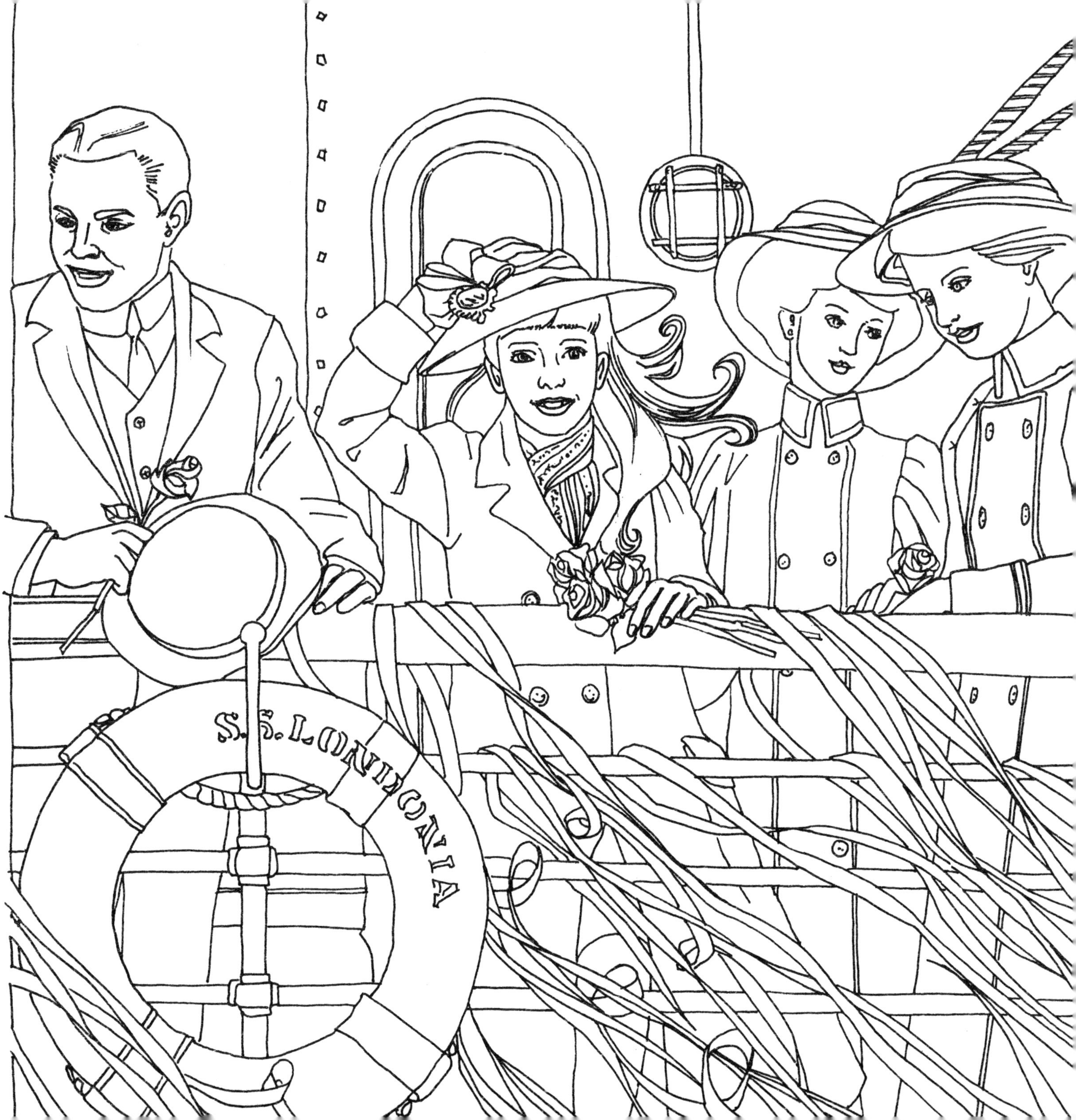
S.S. LONICONIA

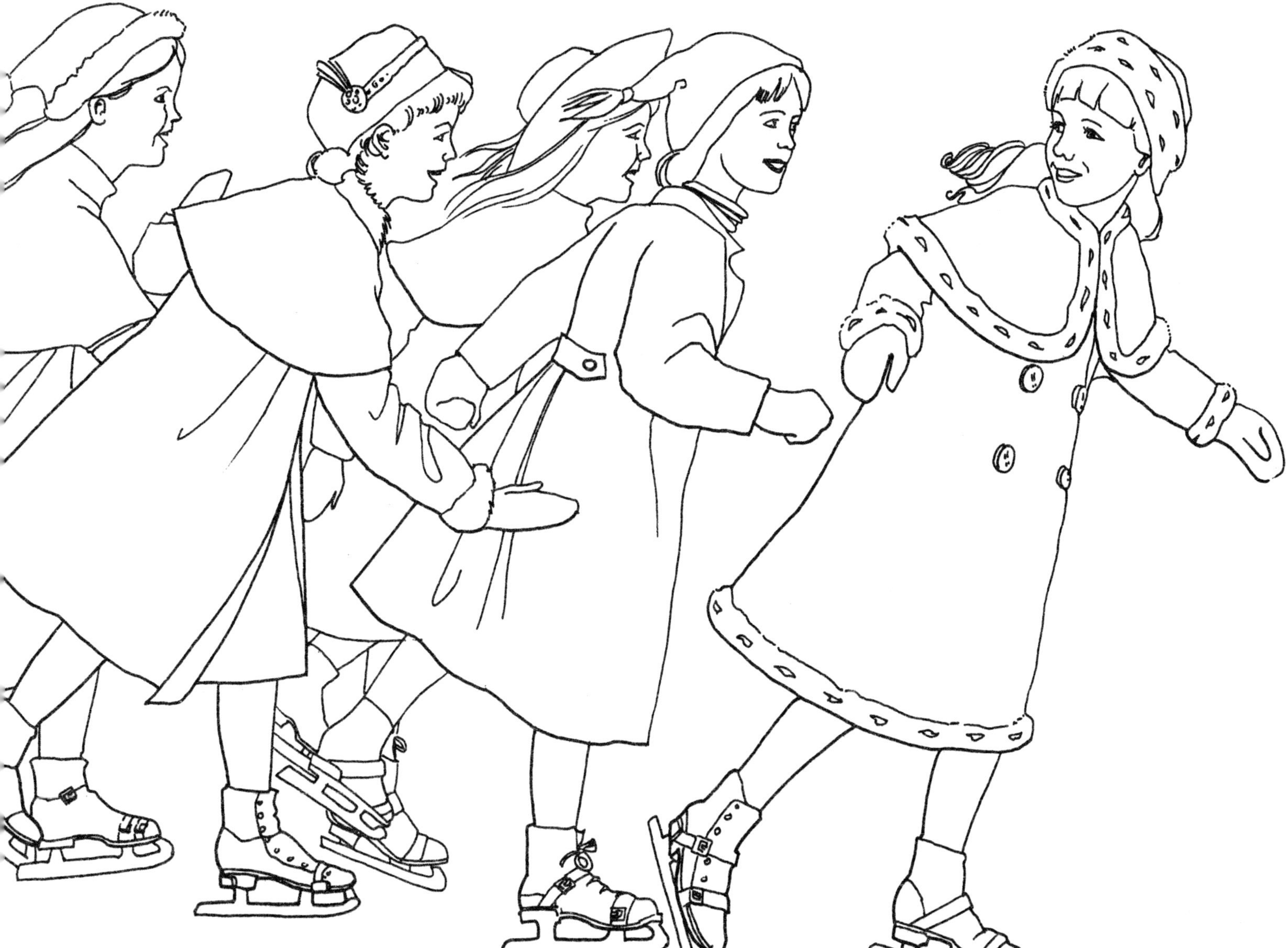

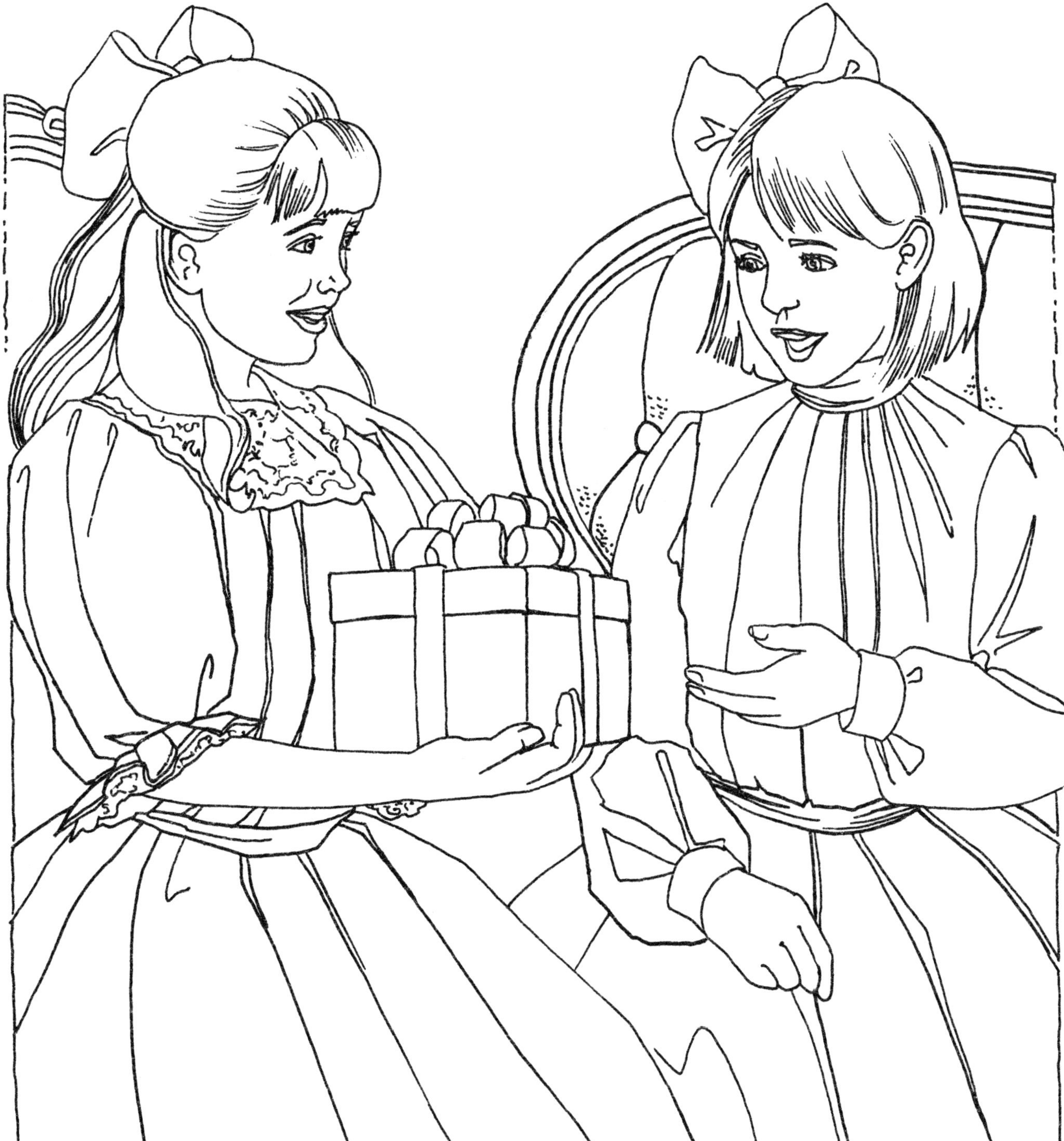

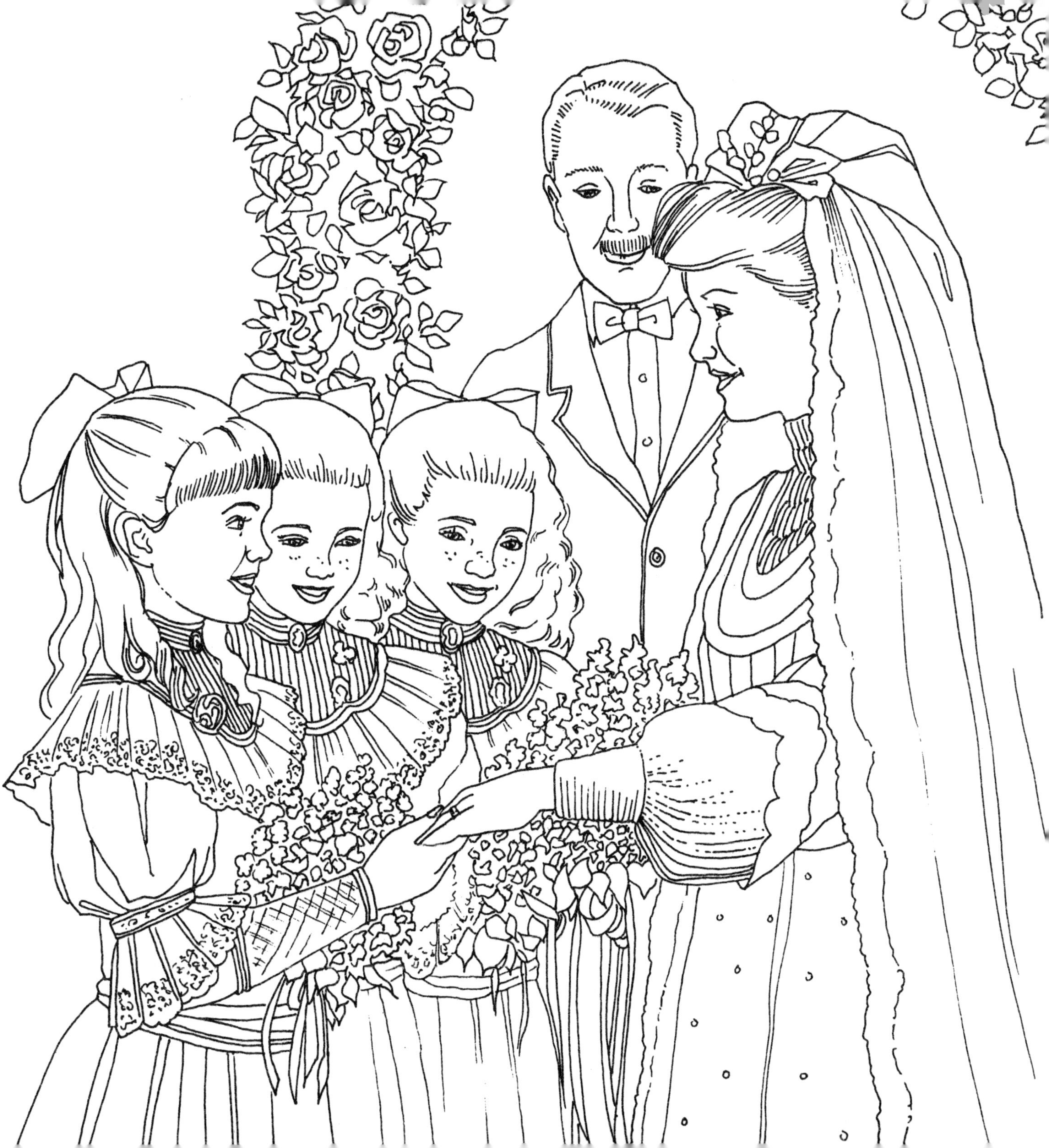